DAVID LANZ & GARY STROUTSOS

spirit romance

ISBN 1-4234-0503-X

HAL•LEONARD®
CORPORATION

7777 W. BLUEMOUND RD. P.O. BOX 13819 MILWAUKEE, WI 53213

Visit Hal Leonard Online at
www.halleonard.com

Visit David Lanz Online at
www.DavidLanz.com

Visit Gary Stroutsos Online at
www.GaryStroutsos.com

introduction

The music of *Spirit Romance* was composed and recorded primarily for piano and flute. However, this transcription can be played two ways: as a work for solo piano, or performed as piano and flute duets.

Playing as written for solo piano, you have the option to add in the flute melody, which is written above the piano part. (The combination of these two parts may best reflect the original recording.)

Listen to the *Spirit Romance* CD and you will hear the distinctive style of pianist David Lanz and master World flutist, Gary Stroutsos, on the ancient Chinese bamboo flute known as the Xiao. The flute transcription herein, however, is written for the traditional concert C flute for ease of access.

If you would like to hear song samples from the original recording they may be found at http://www.davidlanz.com/spirit.htm

(FROM THE CD'S INTRODUCTION)

"The Zen-like quality of the title, *Spirit Romance*, is meant to be open for interpretation by the listener. Imbued with the healing nature of the lush natural world of the Pacific Northwest, where the recording was made, and informed in part with the musical legacy of our world's indigenous peoples… at once romantic, mysterious, and introspective, this music emanates directly from the heart, soul, and hands of its creators.

We now invite our listeners to go with us… deep into this musical landscape, and into the world of *Spirit Romance*."

— David Lanz

THE FLUTE PART IN *SPIRIT ROMANCE*

With its origins dating back 2000 years to the Shang dynasty, the xiao flute frequently was used to express melancholy and peaceful moods as it was coupled with the Chinese gugin (a zither type instrument). A notched flute, the Chinese xiao produces a sound similar in volume to a recorder, but with the tone quality of a bamboo flute.

This publication is intended to assist musicians in exploring the performance dimensions of the compositions in *Spirit Romance*. The manuscript includes performance markings to facilitate a convincing performance imitating the xiao flute. Recommended guidelines include specific dynamics and phrasing, as well as the use of various styles of tone color and vibrato – therefore flutists using modern type metal flutes are encouraged to avoid traditional tonal techniques.

The xiao flute tone produces an exquisite sound with subtle nuances and overtones, requiring modern day flutists to manipulate the air stream for varying color as well as contrasting textures ranging from hollow to vibrant. Some flutists may even wish to perform sections an octave higher in the event that the low register becomes tiresome.

David Lanz's music easily lends itself to an improvisatory style of harmony and expression in *Spirit Romance*. Gary Stroutsos' flute improvisations successfully enhance David Lanz's poetic melodic lines with stylistically embellished musical responses, making these beautiful tone studies and works suitable to recital programs.

— Catherine Thompson, flutist and editor
  The American Flute Guild
  www.americanfluteguild.com

SERENADA

By DAVID LANZ
and GARY STROUTSOS

Slowly, very expressively

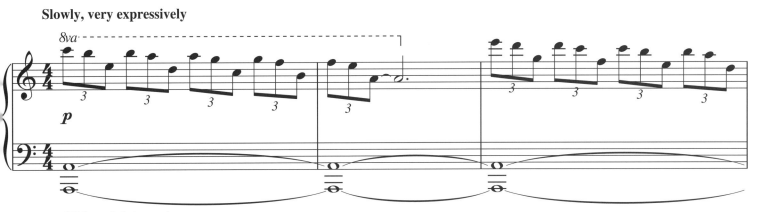

With pedal throughout

(8vb)

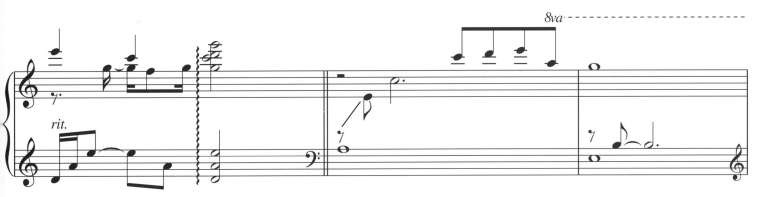

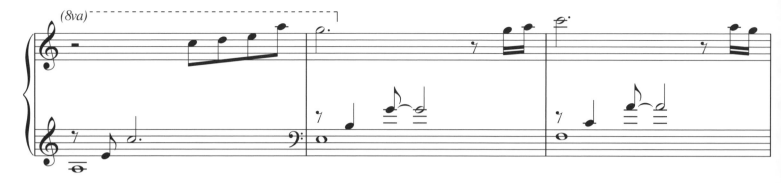

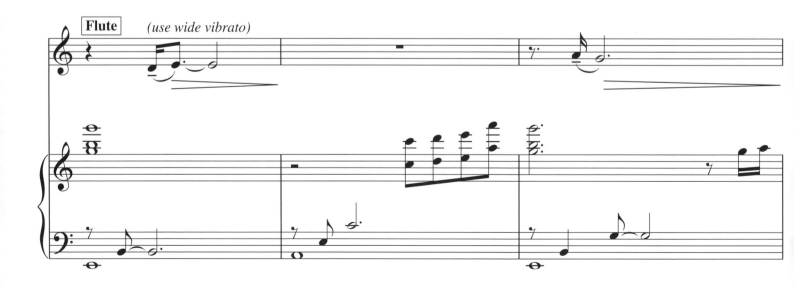

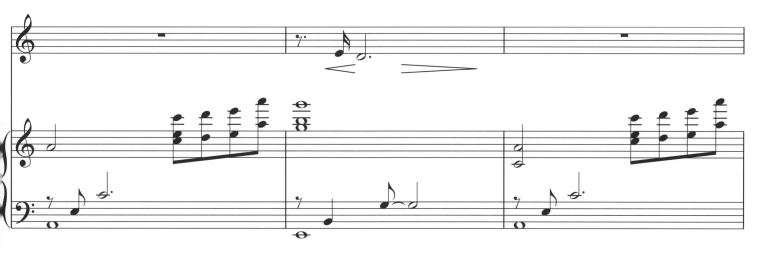

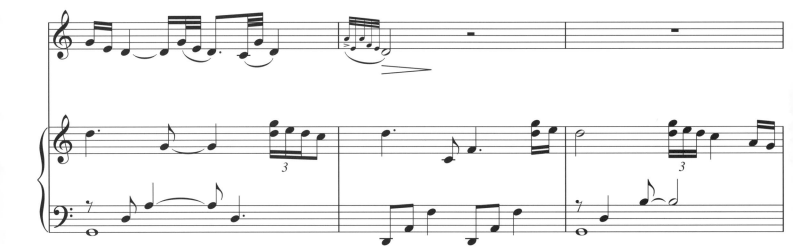

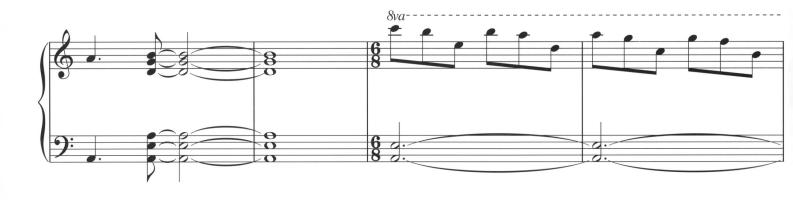

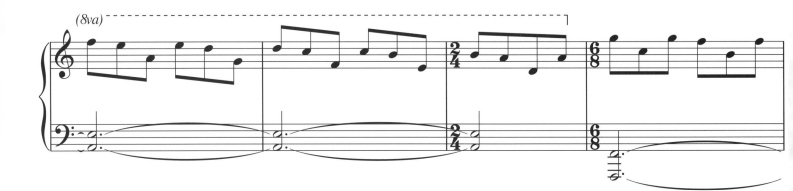

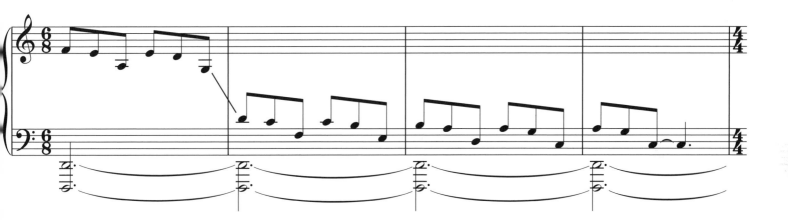

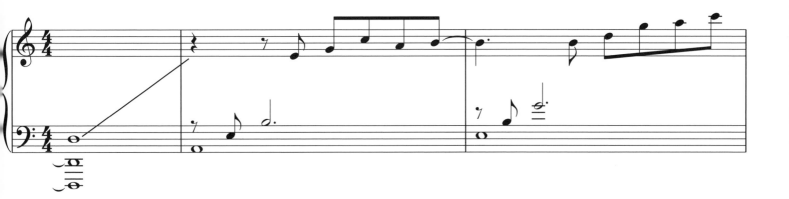

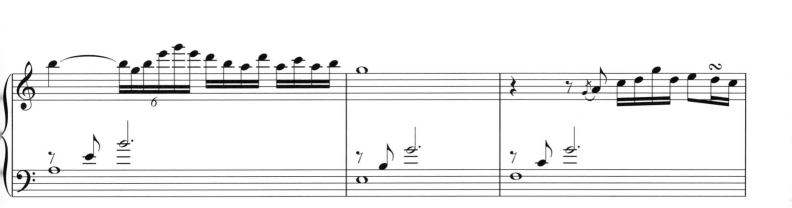

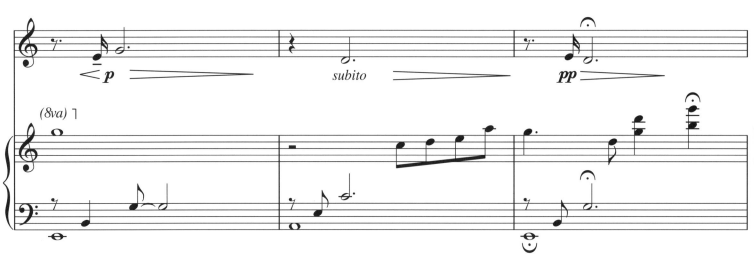

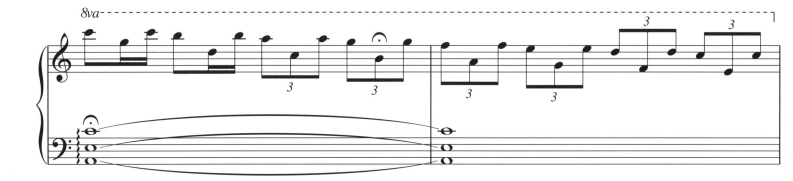

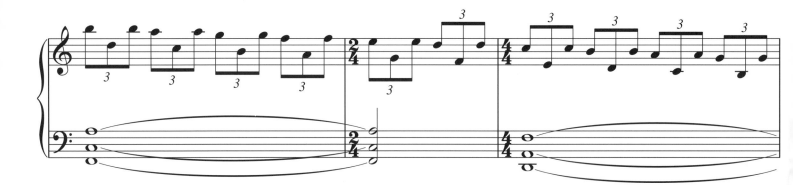

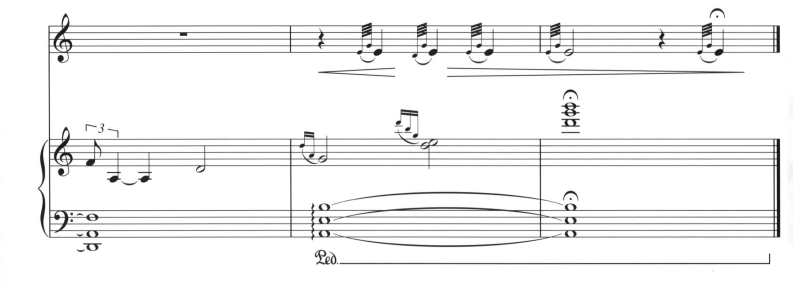

SATORI

By DAVID LANZ
and GARY STROUTSOS

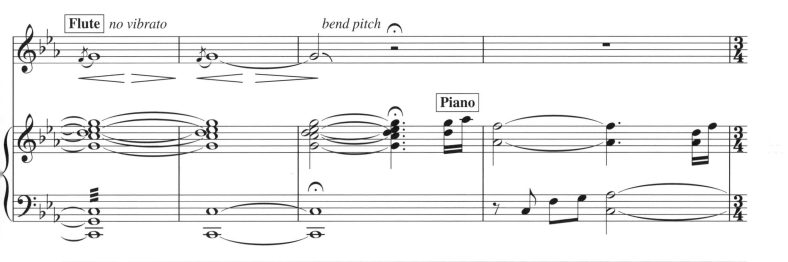

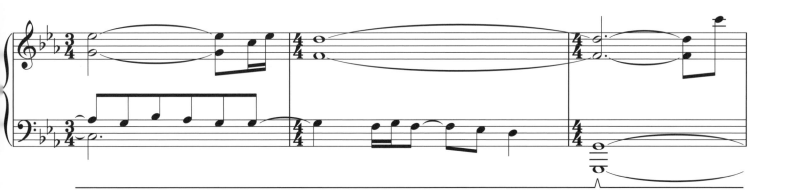

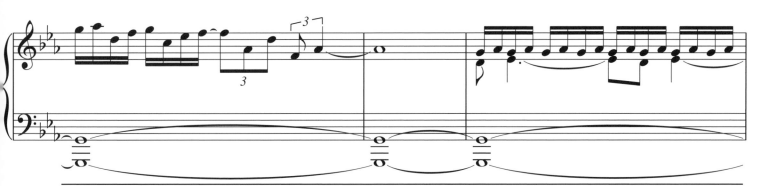

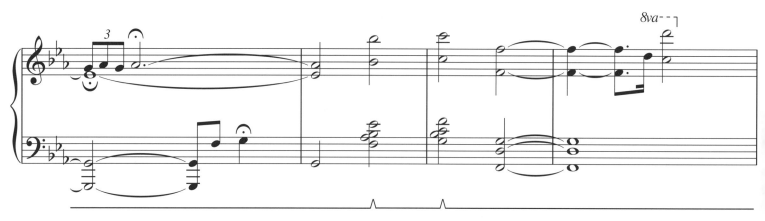

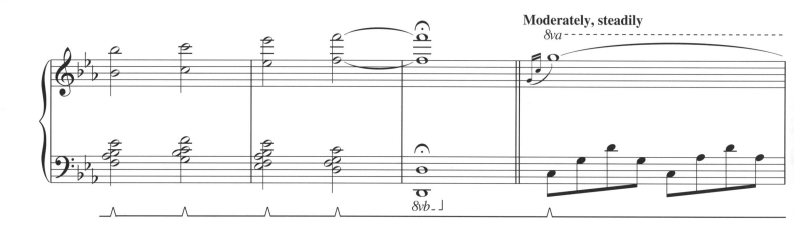

Moderately, steadily

(Pedal simile)

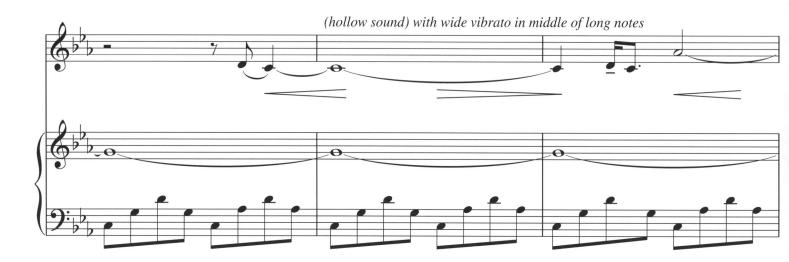

(hollow sound) with wide vibrato in middle of long notes

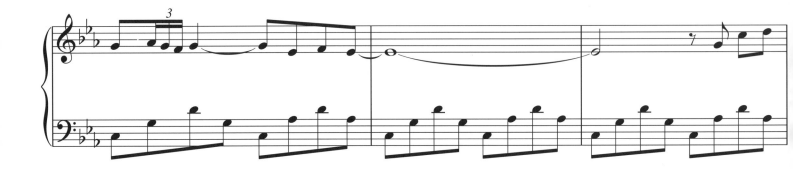

Slowly, very freely

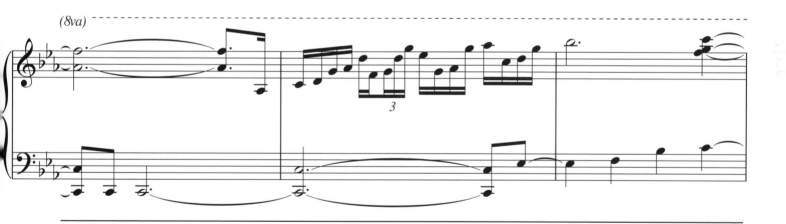

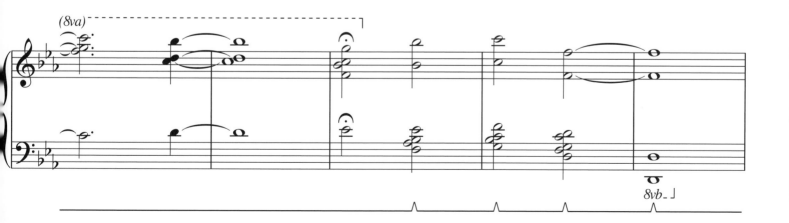

Tempo II

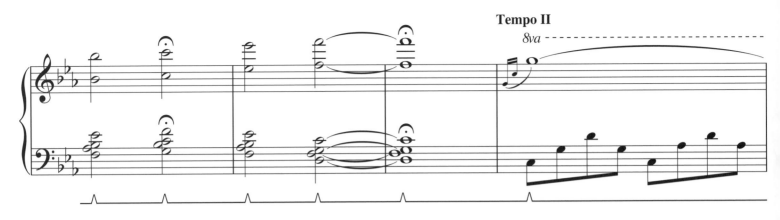

(Pedal simile)

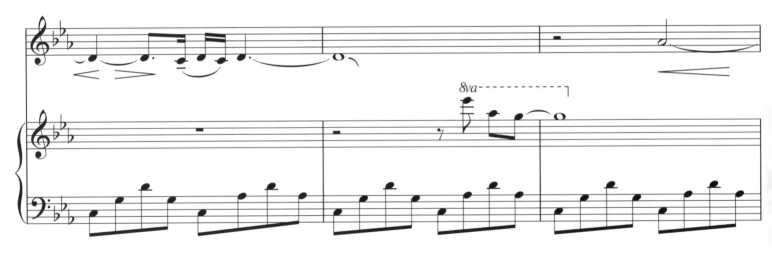

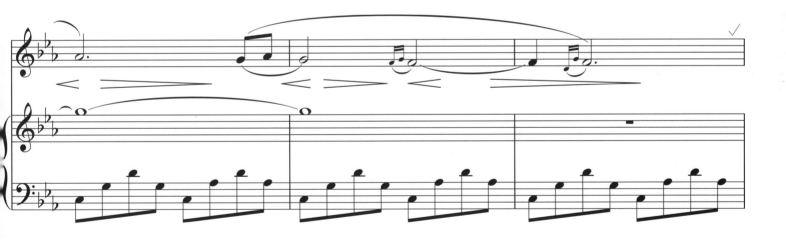

Slowly, very freely

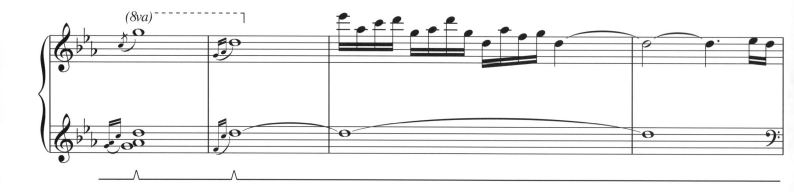

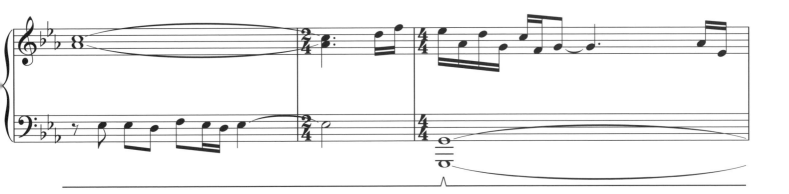

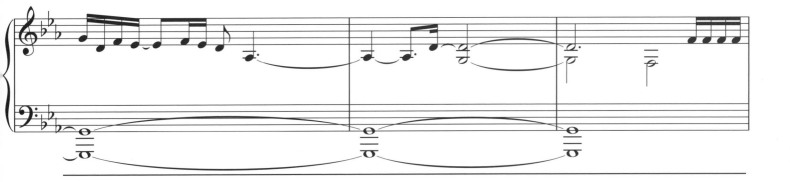

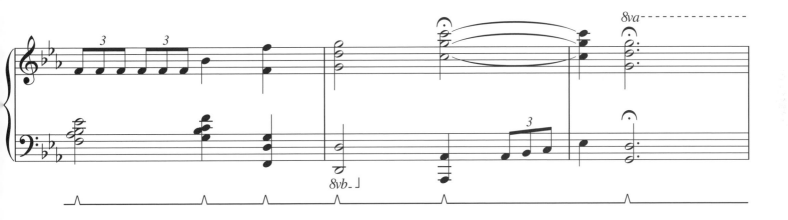

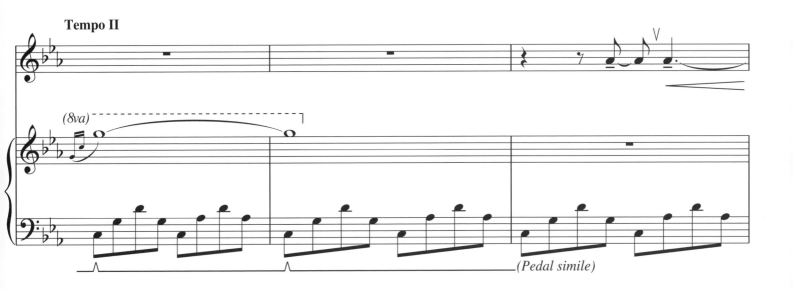

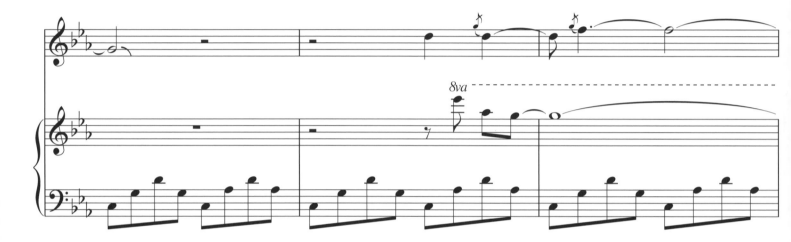

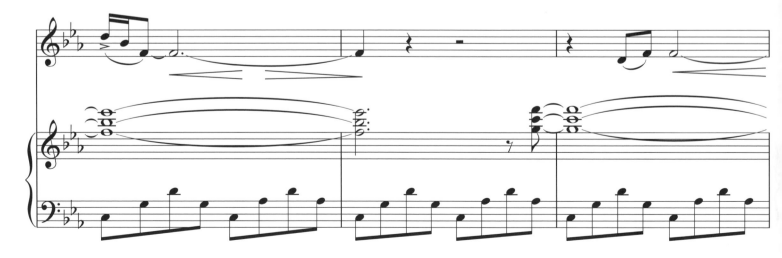

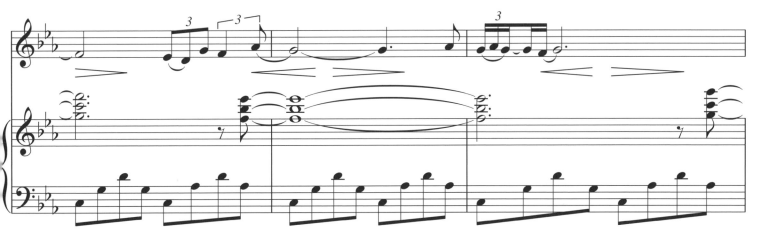

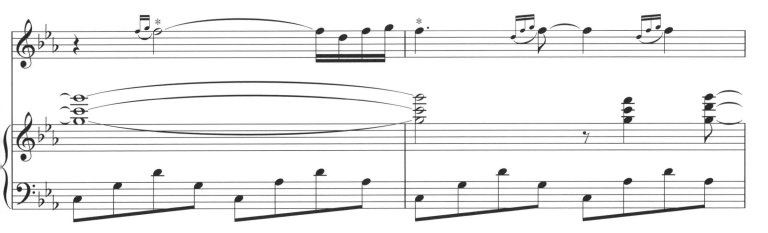

(switch to Thumb B♭ fingering in this measure)

* Half cover R.H. 1st finger.

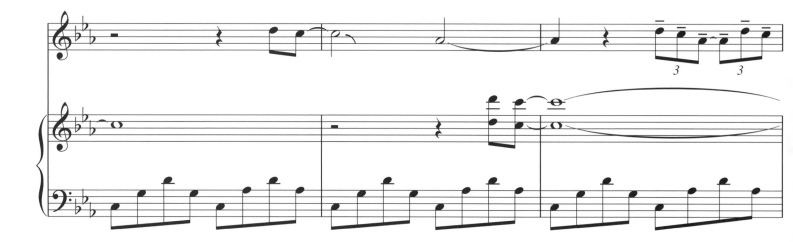

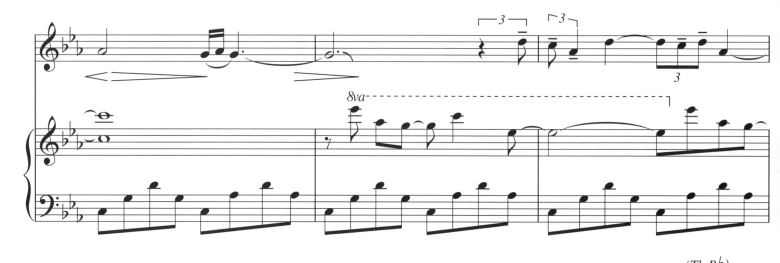

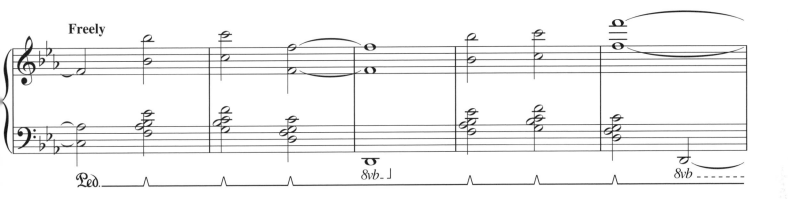

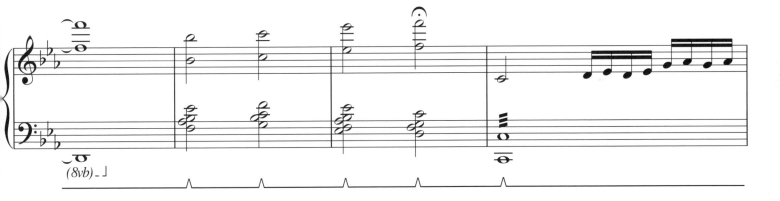

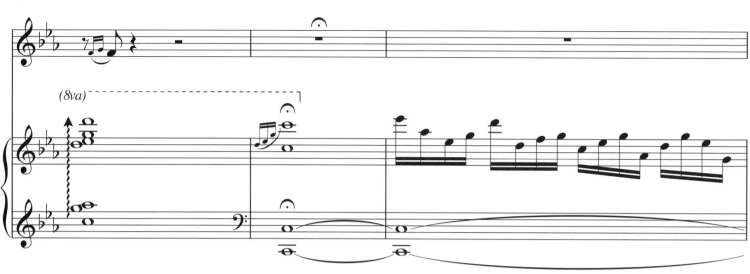

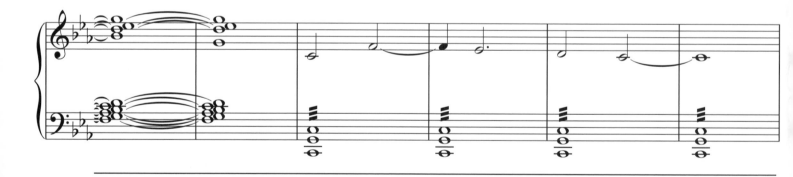

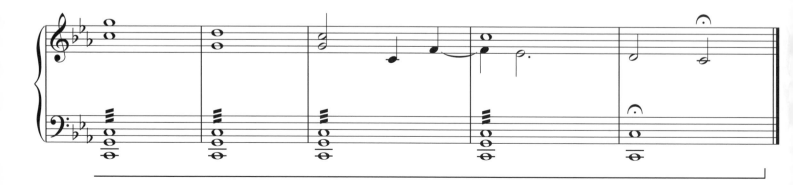

BETWEEN WORLDS

By DAVID LANZ

Moderately slow, very expressively

p

rit.

a tempo

With pedal throughout

a tempo

rit.

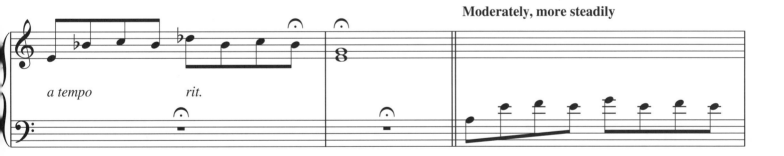

a tempo

rit.

Moderately, more steadily

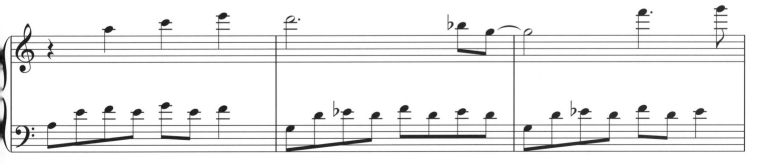

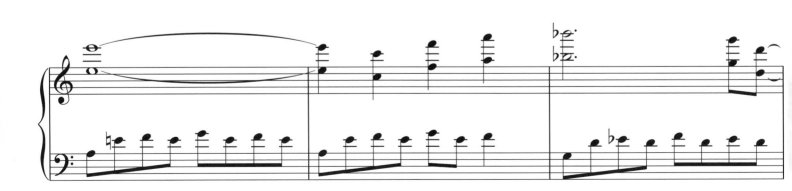

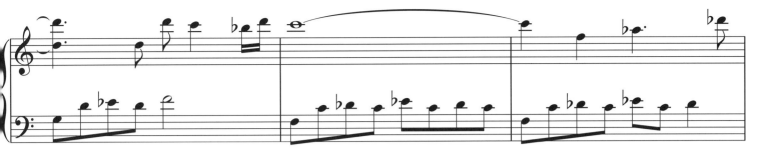

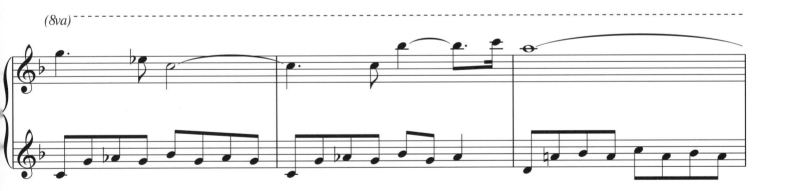

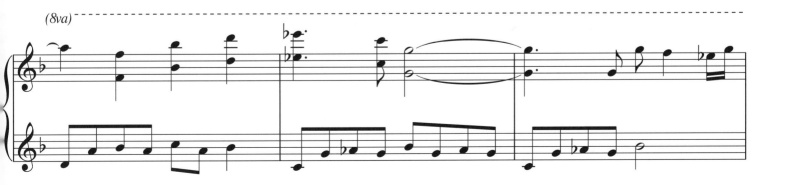

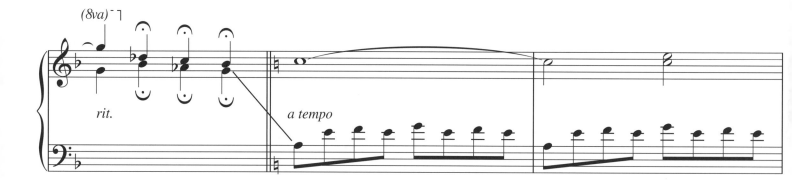

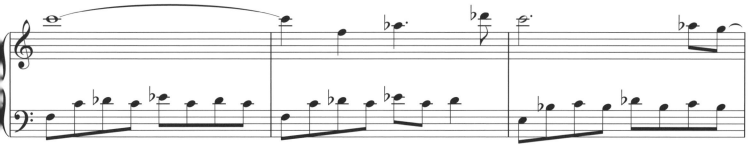

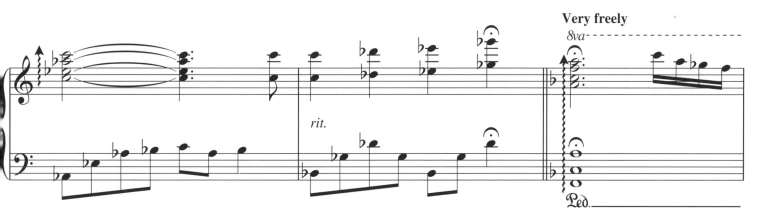

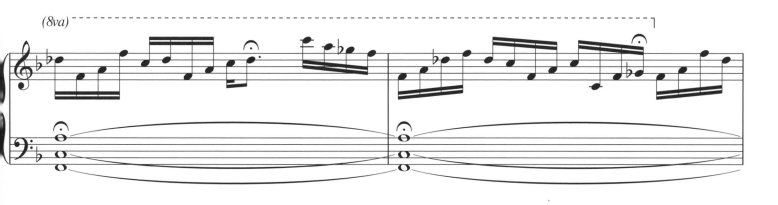

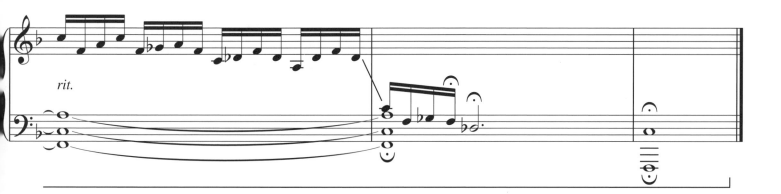

OGUERRE
(The Blue Largo Arrangement)

Written by GILBERTO VALDES

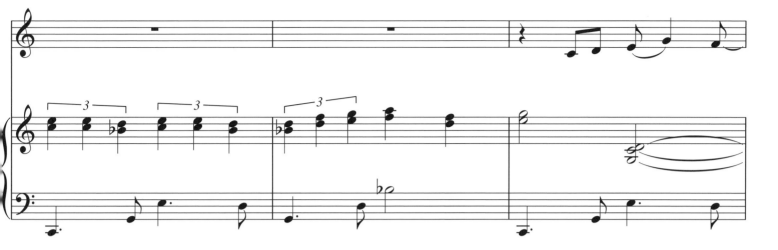

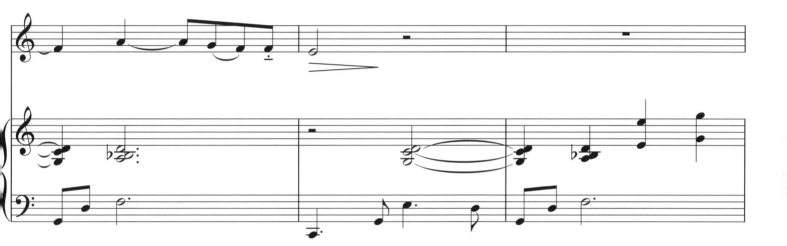

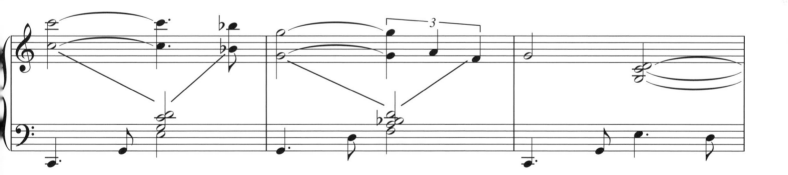

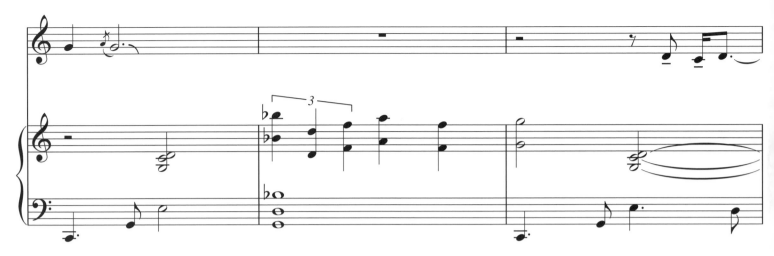

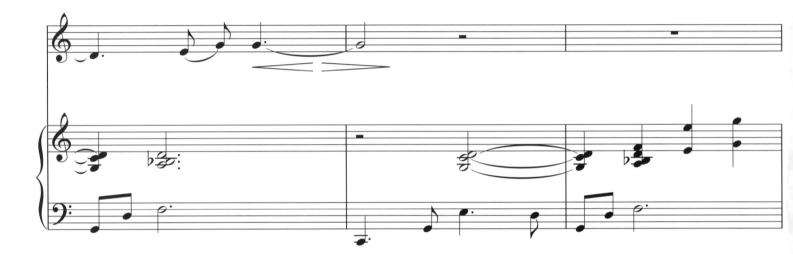

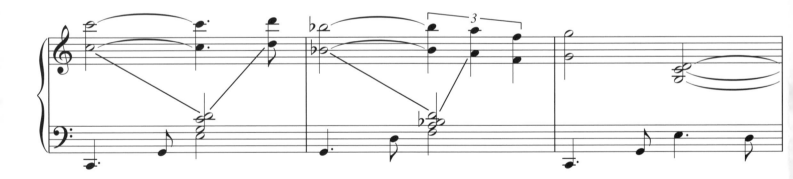

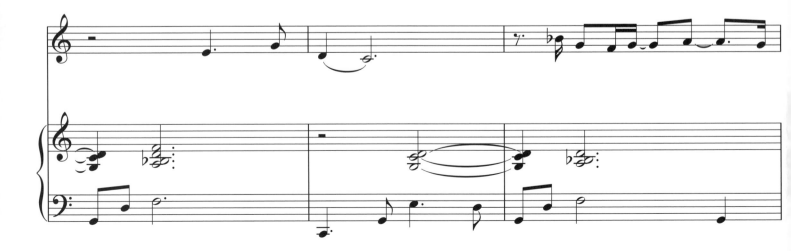

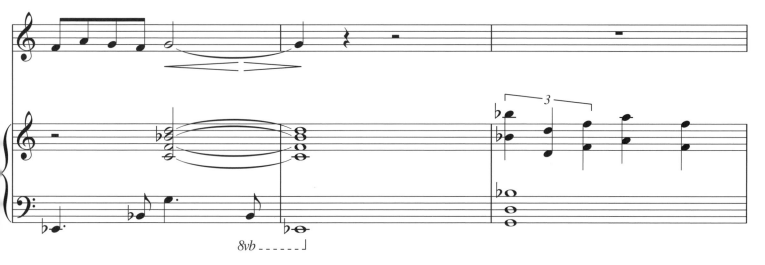

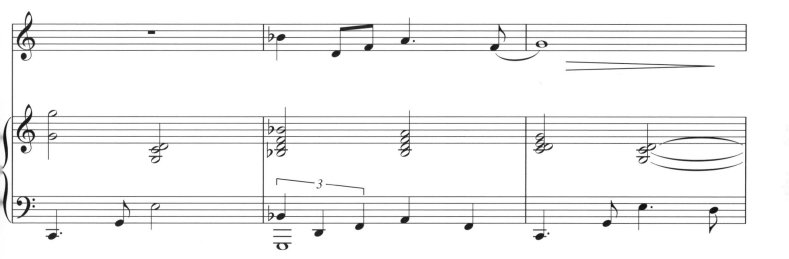

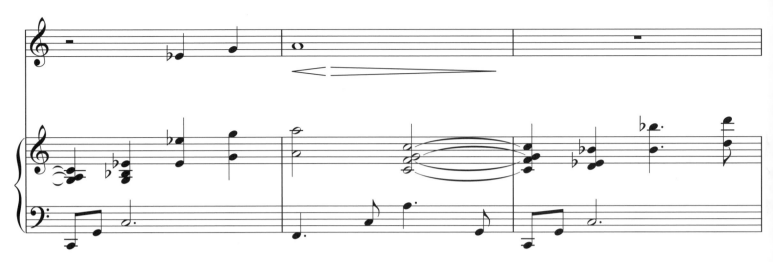

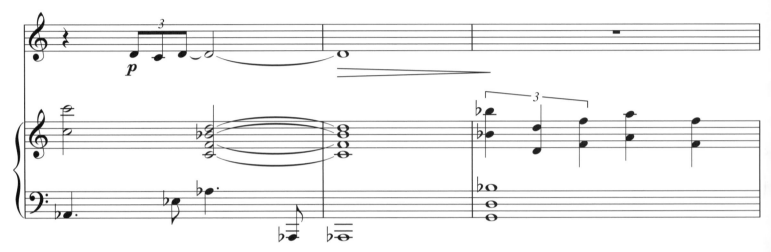

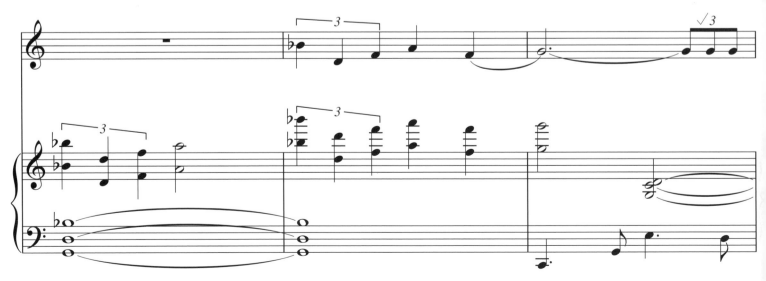

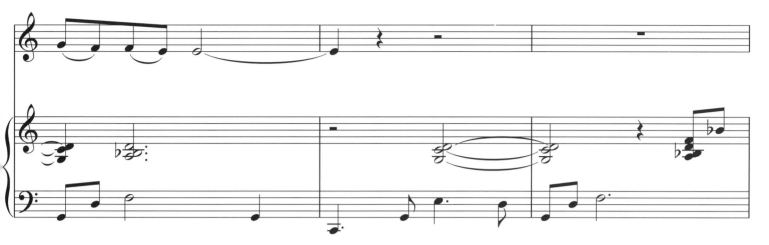

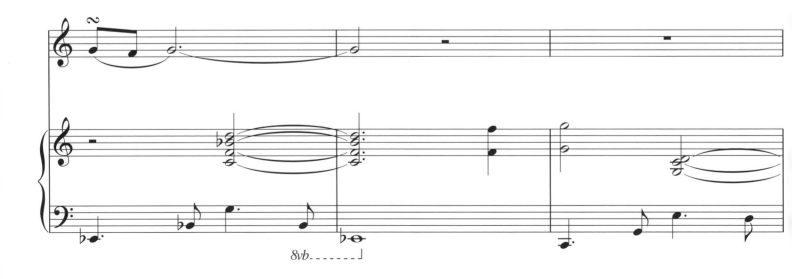

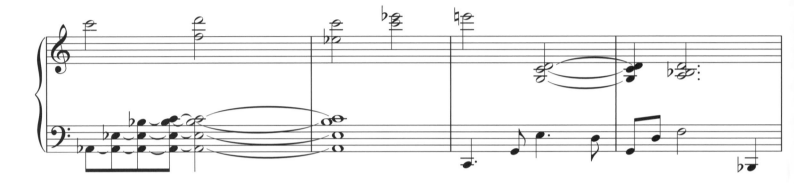

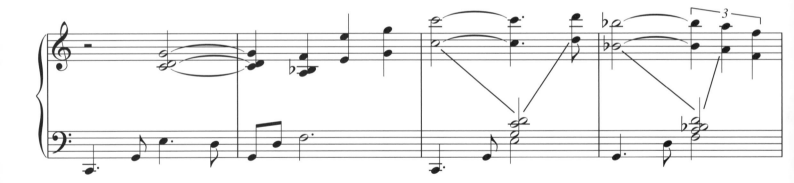

Improvise freely to end

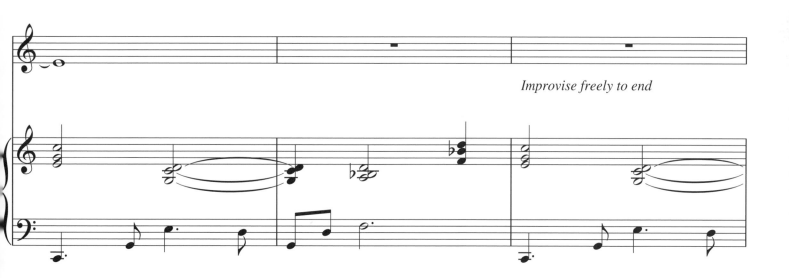

Repeat ad lib. and Fade | **Optional Ending**

SPIRIT ROMANCE

By DAVID LANZ
and GARY STROUTSOS

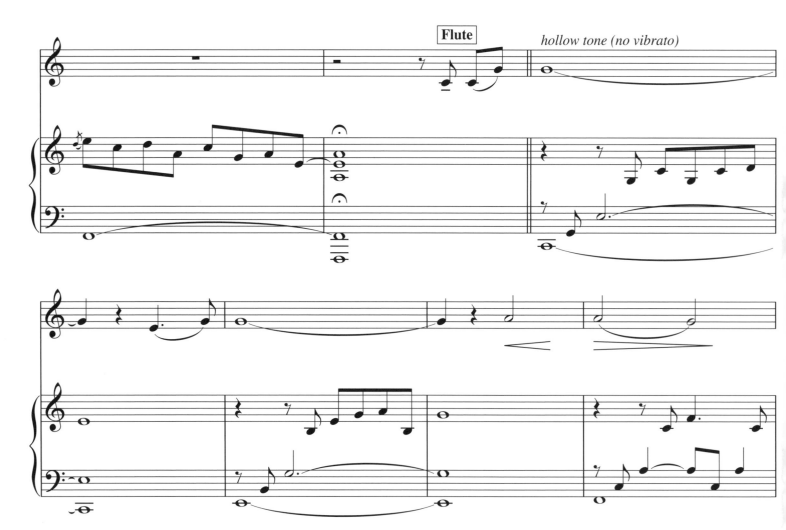

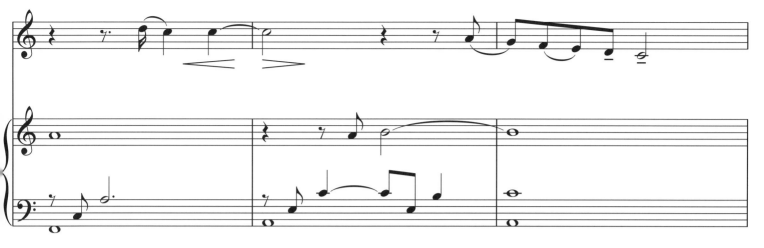

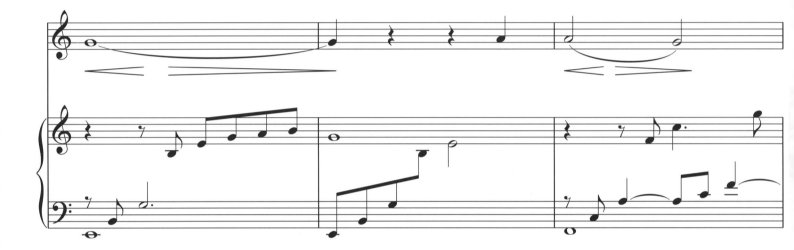

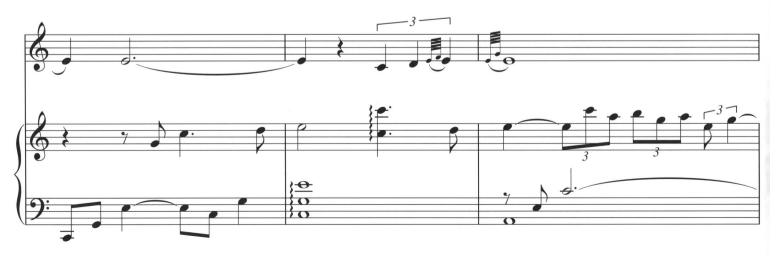

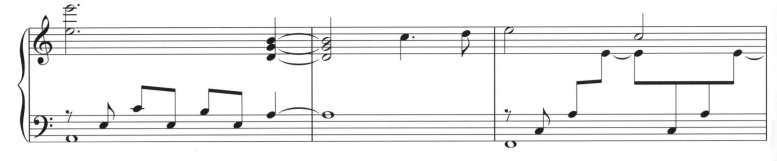

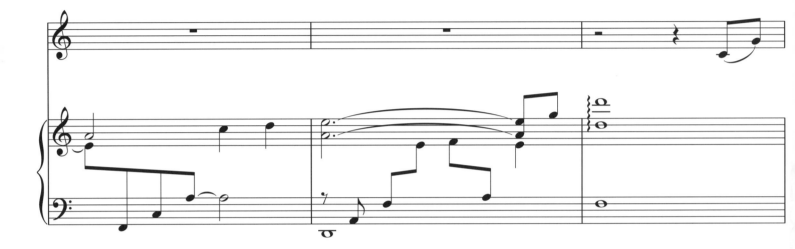

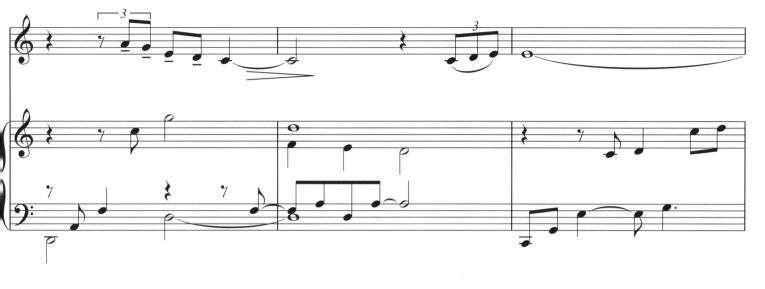

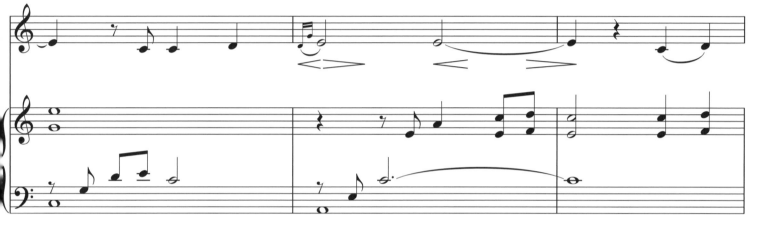

Very slowly **Tempo I**

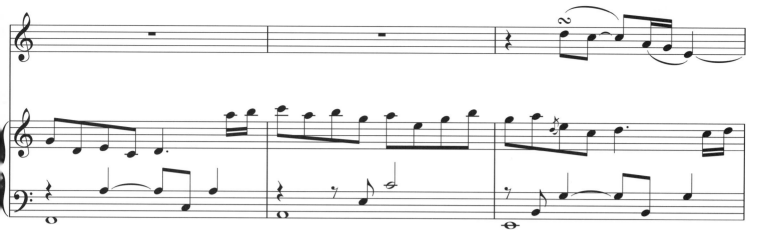

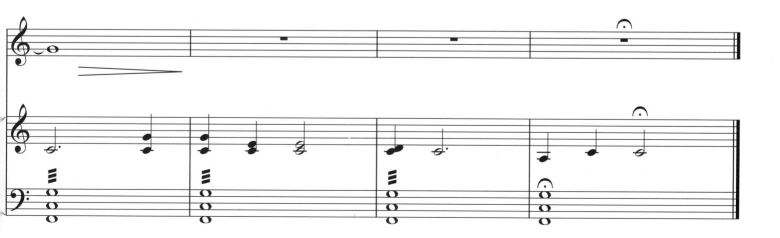

Unaccompanied Flute

SOLILOQUY

By GARY STROUTSOS

Moderately slow, freely

RETURN TO ALTAIR
(A Suite in Five Parts)
A Distant Light

By DAVID LANZ
and GARY STROUTSOS

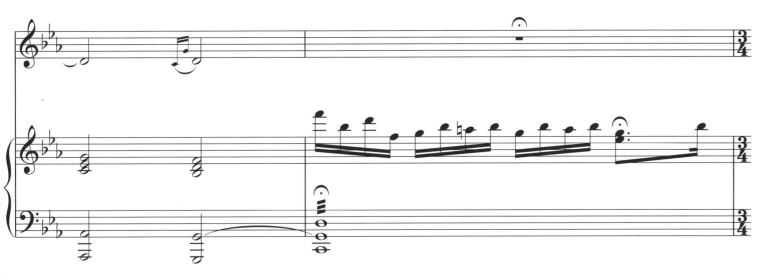

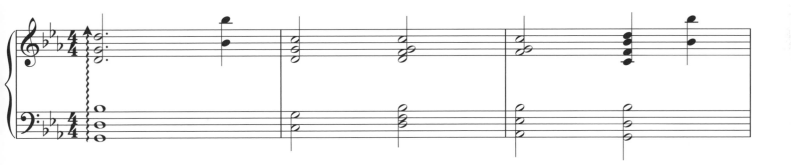

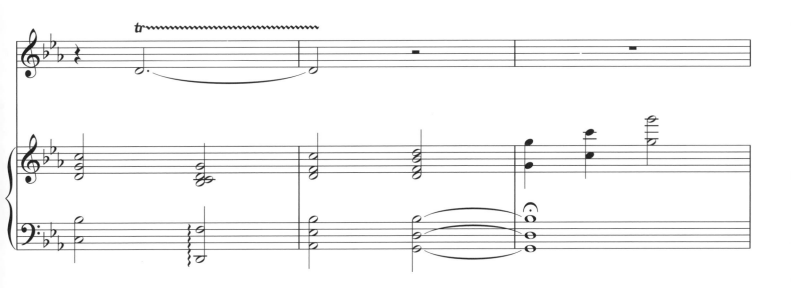

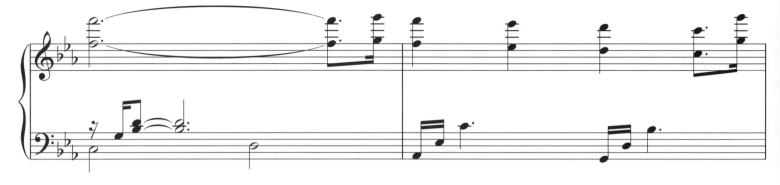

Segue to "Dreams of Altair"

Dreams Of Altair

By DAVID LANZ
and GARY LANZ

Moderately fast

With pedal throughout

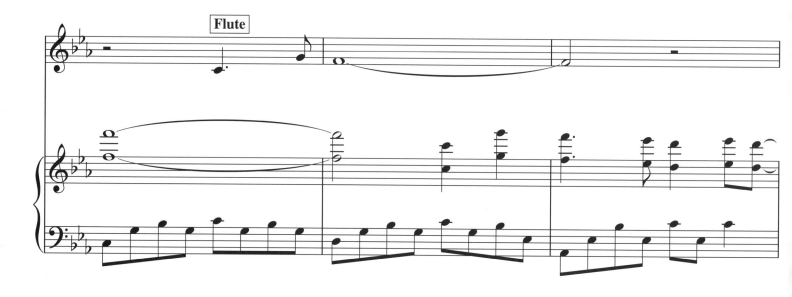

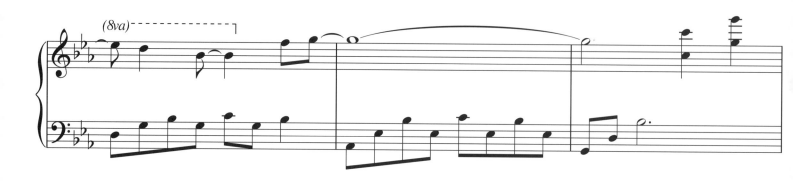

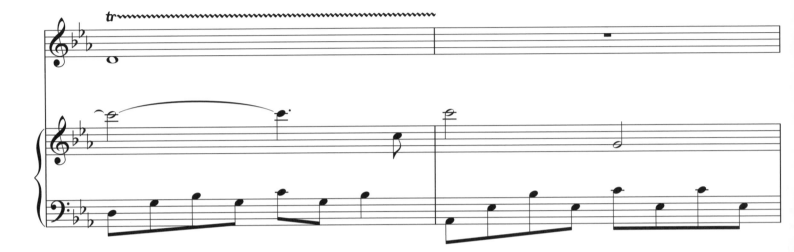

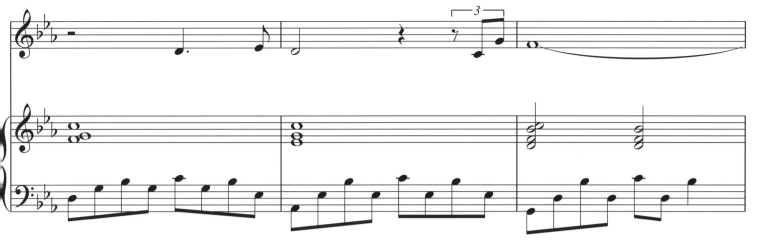

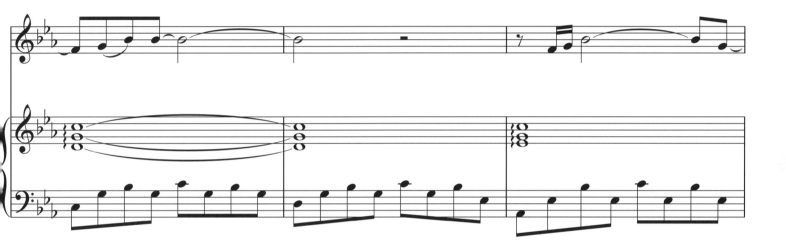

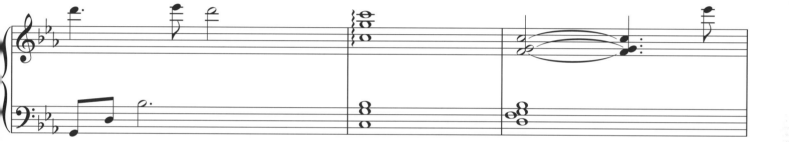

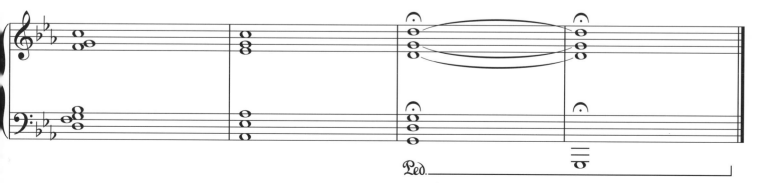

Segue to "Contemplation"

Contemplation

By DAVID LANZ
and GARY LANZ

Moderately fast

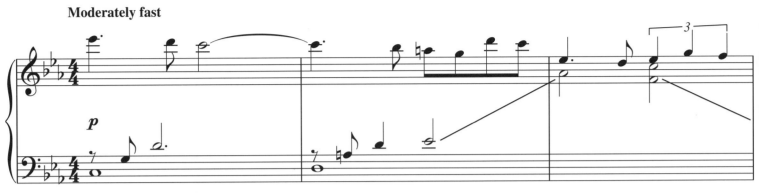

With pedal throughout

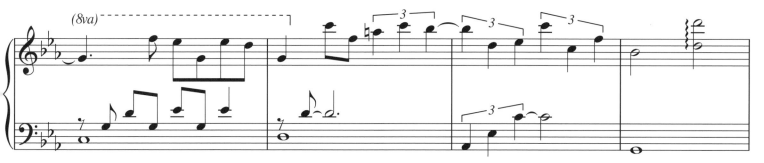

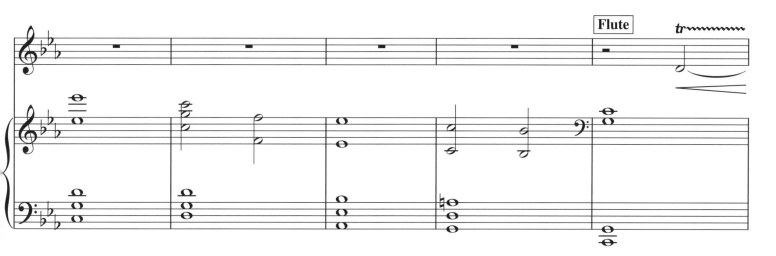

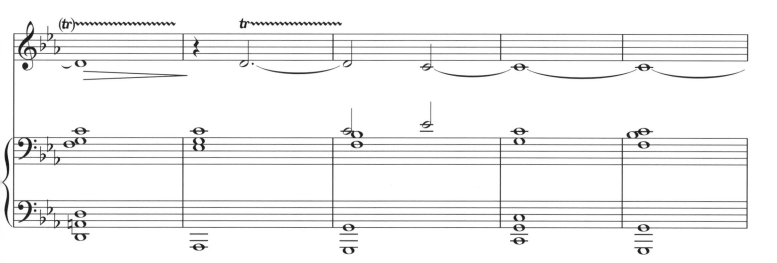

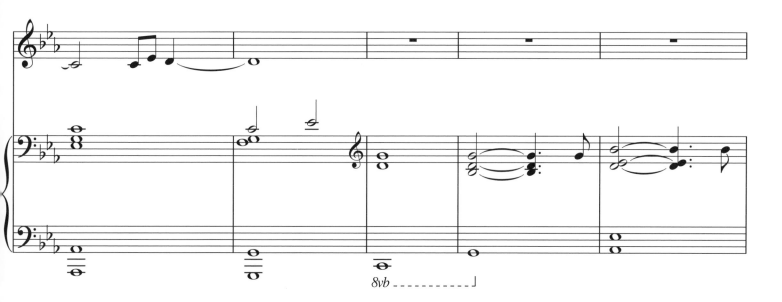

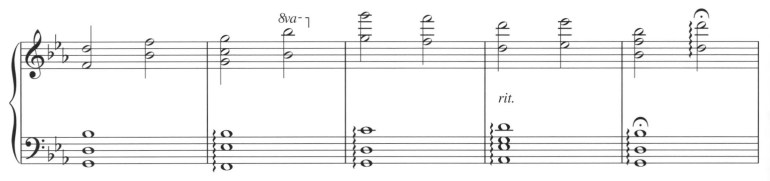

Tempo I

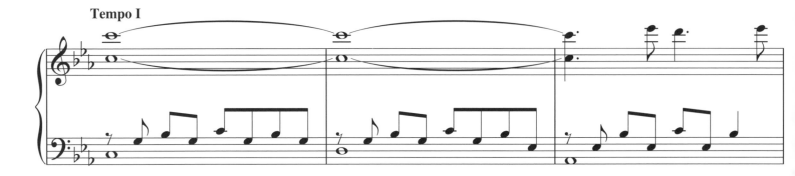

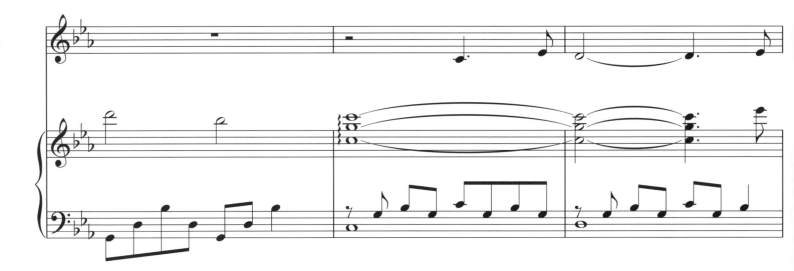

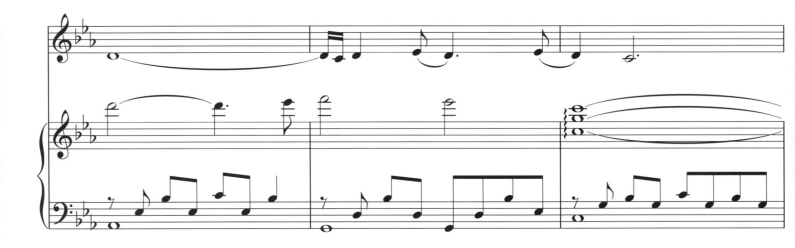

Slowly, very freely

rit.

8va

8vb

(8va)

(8vb)

(8vb)

8vb

8va

8va

Segue to "Compassion"

Compassion

By DAVID LANZ
and GARY STROUTSOS

Very slowly, expressively

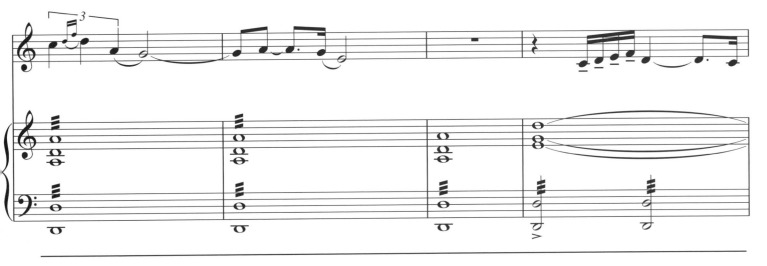

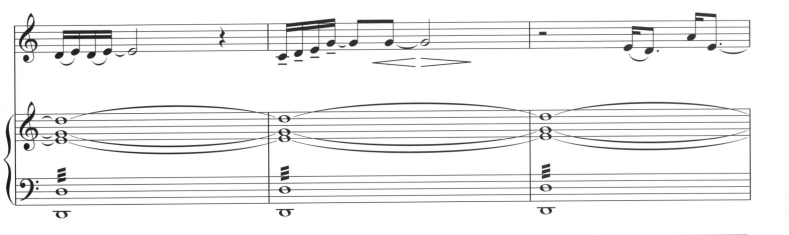

Segue to "The Return"

The Return

By DAVID LANZ
and GARY STROUTSOS

Moderately fast

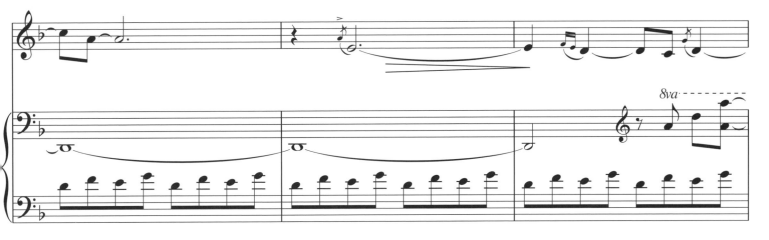

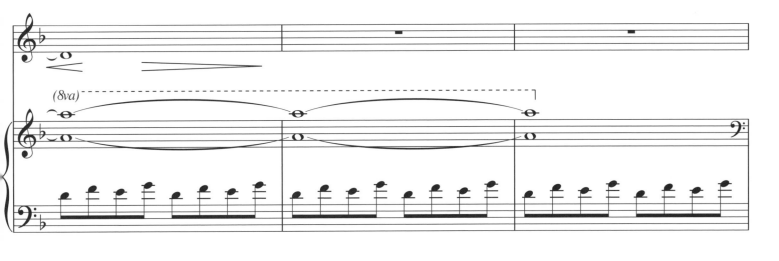

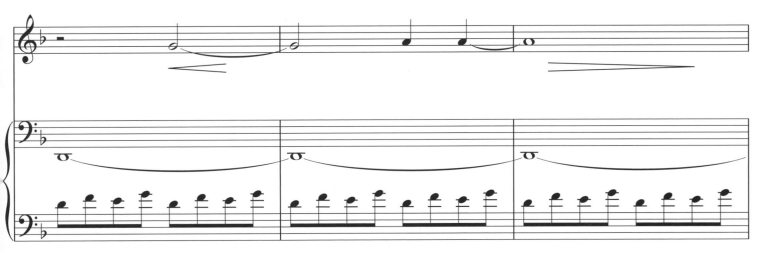

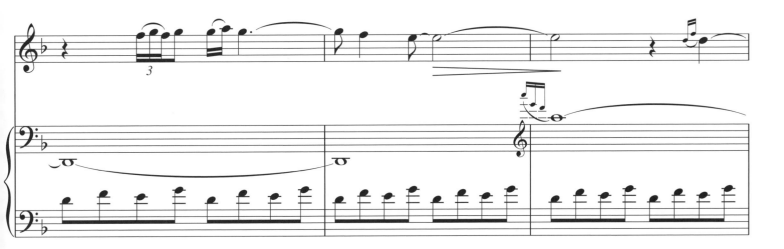

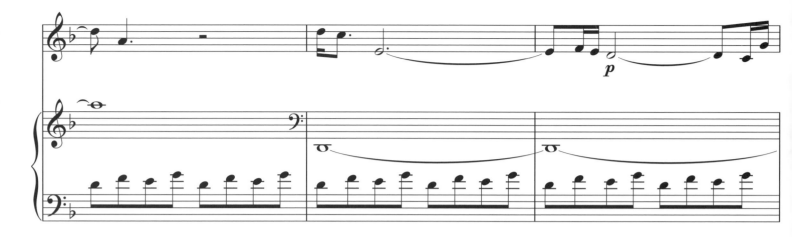

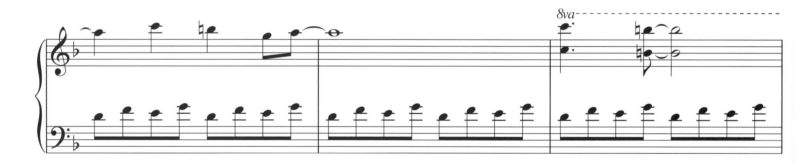

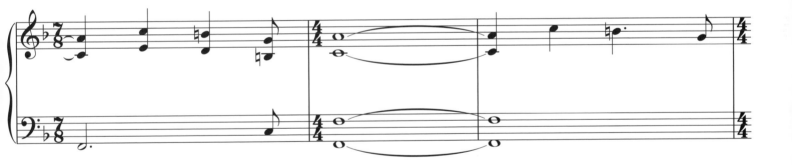

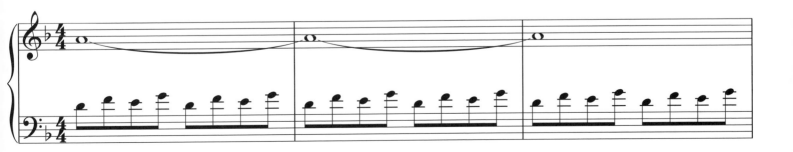

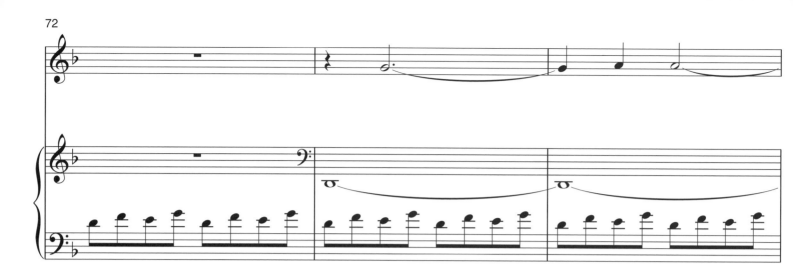

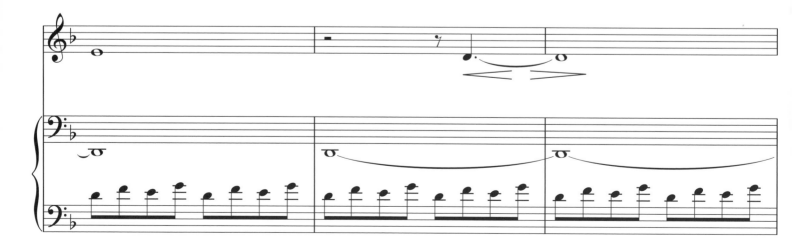

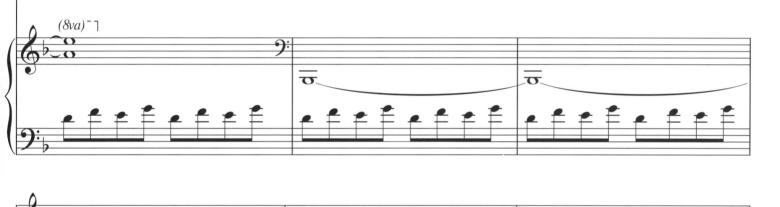
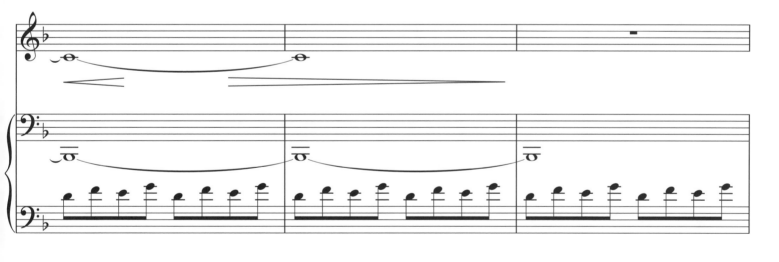
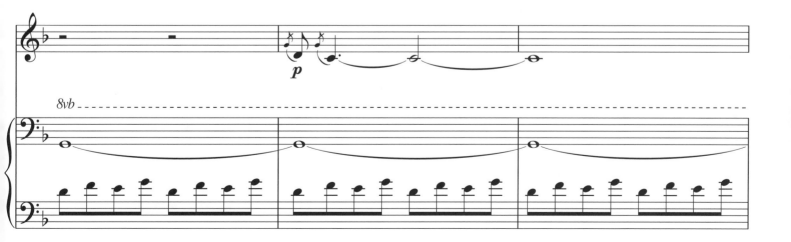

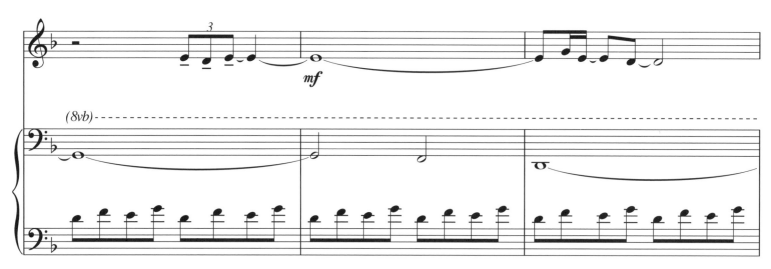

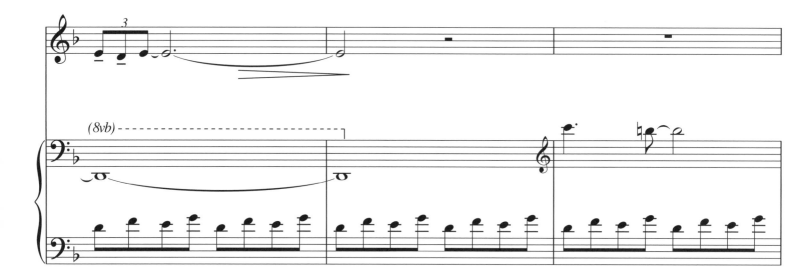

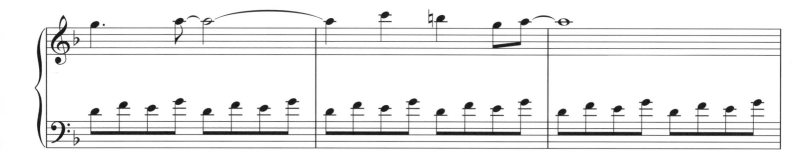

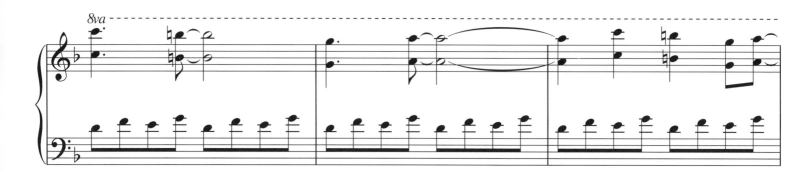

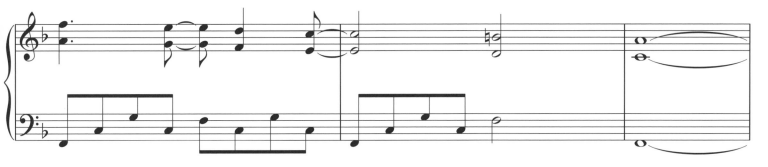

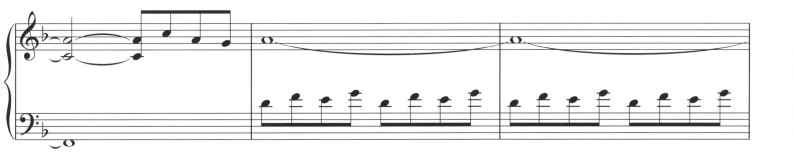

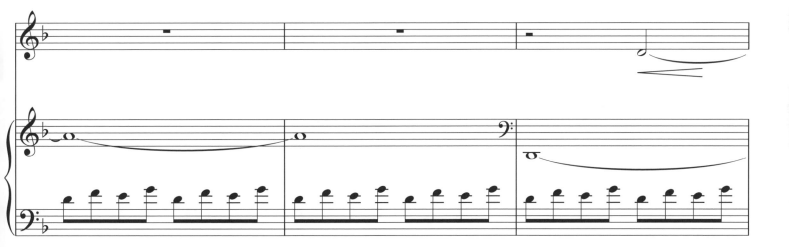

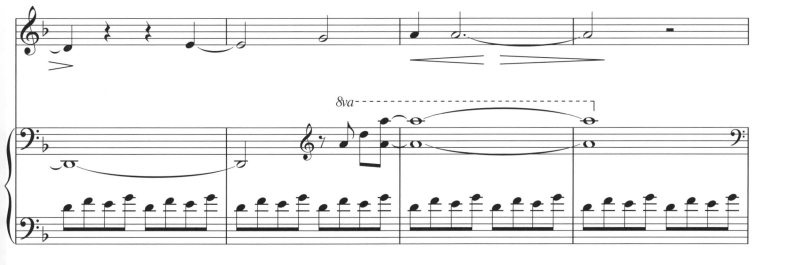

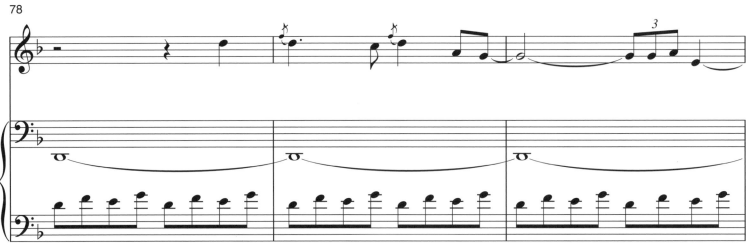

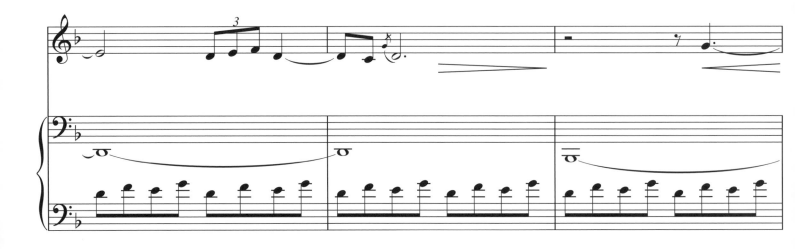

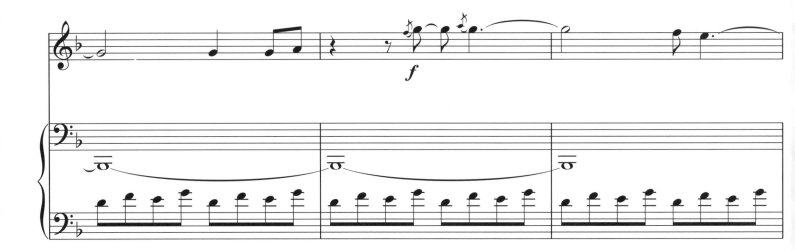

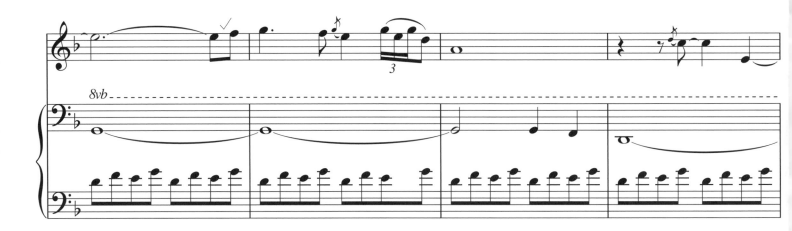

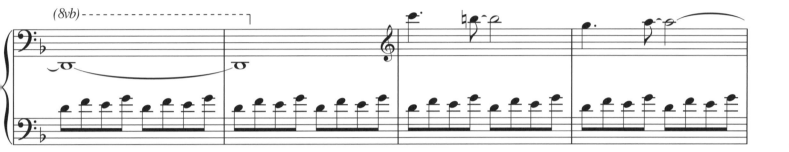

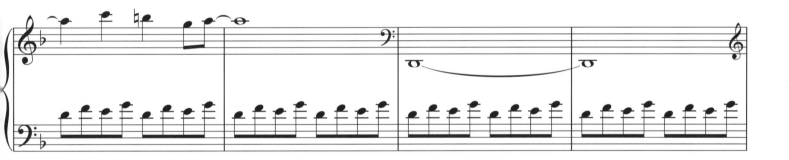

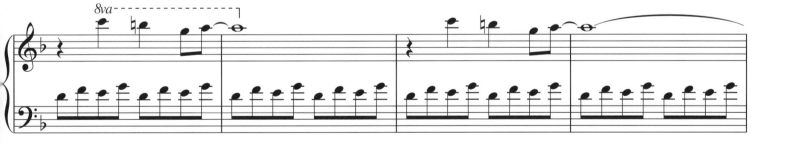

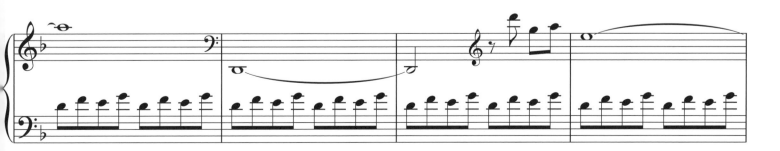

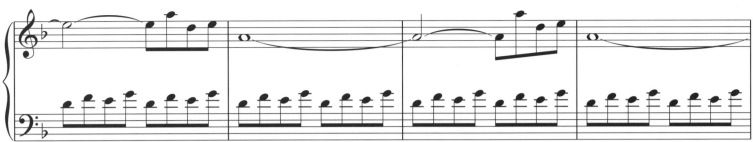

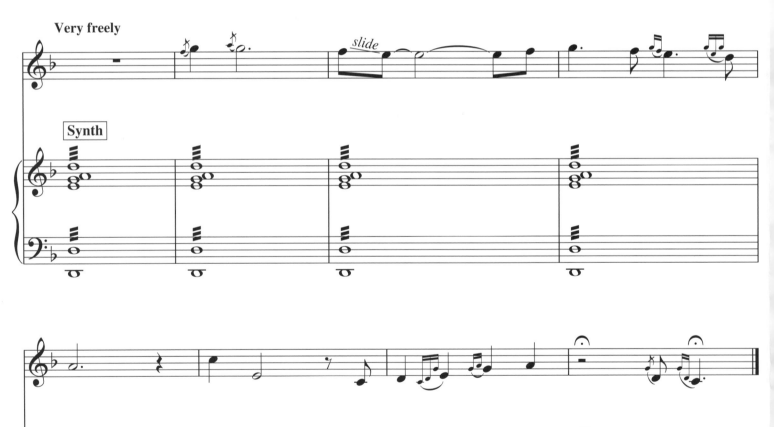

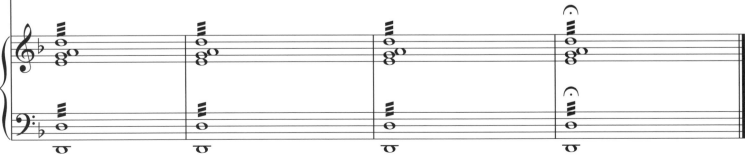